Evidence
Book

Whatever problems you may be facing, it is important to record evidence in order to build a case against the other party, or to assist with any complaint you might be intending to make.

This book provides a central record of events, conversations, incidents and other circumstances which will build to help you prove your case, whatever your reasons for doing so.

It is important to record the date and time of each event.

Record details of any photographs or documents and importantly, where these can be found.

Complete the details of each event carefully and accurately.

Write down the names and other details (if known) of any witnesses to each event.

Sign it at the bottom.

| Date/Time |
| What happened? |

Other related evidence, such as photographs or documents, including where these are stored.

Witnessed by

Signed as a true record of events

Date/Time
What happened?

Other related evidence, such as photographs or documents, including where these are stored.

Witnessed by

Signed as a true record of events

Date/Time
What happened?

Other related evidence, such as photographs or documents, including where these are stored.

Witnessed by

Signed as a true record of events

Date/Time
What happened?

Other related evidence, such as photographs or documents, including where these are stored.

Witnessed by

Signed as a true record of events

Date/Time
What happened?

Other related evidence, such as photographs or documents, including where these are stored.

Witnessed by

Signed as a true record of events

Date/Time
What happened?

Other related evidence, such as photographs or documents, including where these are stored.

Witnessed by

Signed as a true record of events

Date/Time
What happened?

Other related evidence, such as photographs or documents, including where these are stored.

Witnessed by

Signed as a true record of events

Date/Time
What happened?

Other related evidence, such as photographs or documents, including where these are stored.

Witnessed by

Signed as a true record of events

Date/Time
What happened?

Other related evidence, such as photographs or documents, including where these are stored.

Witnessed by

Signed as a true record of events

Date/Time
What happened?

Other related evidence, such as photographs or documents, including where these are stored.

Witnessed by

Signed as a true record of events

Date/Time
What happened?

Other related evidence, such as photographs or documents, including where these are stored.

Witnessed by

Signed as a true record of events

Date/Time
What happened?

Other related evidence, such as photographs or documents, including where these are stored.

Witnessed by

Signed as a true record of events

Date/Time
What happened?

Other related evidence, such as photographs or documents, including where these are stored.

Witnessed by

Signed as a true record of events

Date/Time
What happened?

Other related evidence, such as photographs or documents, including where these are stored.

Witnessed by

Signed as a true record of events

Date/Time
What happened?

Other related evidence, such as photographs or documents, including where these are stored.

Witnessed by

Signed as a true record of events

Date/Time
What happened?

Other related evidence, such as photographs or documents, including where these are stored.

Witnessed by

Signed as a true record of events

Date/Time
What happened?

Other related evidence, such as photographs or documents, including where these are stored.

Witnessed by

Signed as a true record of events

Date/Time
What happened?

Other related evidence, such as photographs or documents, including where these are stored.

Witnessed by

Signed as a true record of events

Date/Time
What happened?

Other related evidence, such as photographs or documents, including where these are stored.

Witnessed by

Signed as a true record of events

Date/Time
What happened?

Other related evidence, such as photographs or documents, including where these are stored.

Witnessed by

Signed as a true record of events

Date/Time
What happened?

Other related evidence, such as photographs or documents, including where these are stored.

Witnessed by

Signed as a true record of events

Date/Time
What happened?

Other related evidence, such as photographs or documents, including where these are stored.

Witnessed by

Signed as a true record of events

Date/Time
What happened?

Other related evidence, such as photographs or documents, including where these are stored.

Witnessed by

Signed as a true record of events

Date/Time
What happened?

Other related evidence, such as photographs or documents, including where these are stored.

Witnessed by

Signed as a true record of events

Date/Time
What happened?

Other related evidence, such as photographs or documents, including where these are stored.

Witnessed by

Signed as a true record of events

Date/Time
What happened?

Other related evidence, such as photographs or documents, including where these are stored.

Witnessed by

Signed as a true record of events

Date/Time
What happened?

Other related evidence, such as photographs or documents, including where these are stored.

Witnessed by

Signed as a true record of events

Date/Time
What happened?

Other related evidence, such as photographs or documents, including where these are stored.

Witnessed by

Signed as a true record of events

Date/Time
What happened?

Other related evidence, such as photographs or documents, including where these are stored.

Witnessed by

Signed as a true record of events

Date/Time
What happened?

Other related evidence, such as photographs
or documents, including where these are
stored.

Witnessed by

Signed as a true record of events

Date/Time
What happened?

Other related evidence, such as photographs or documents, including where these are stored.

Witnessed by

Signed as a true record of events

Date/Time
What happened?

Other related evidence, such as photographs or documents, including where these are stored.

Witnessed by

Signed as a true record of events

Date/Time
What happened?

Other related evidence, such as photographs or documents, including where these are stored.

Witnessed by

Signed as a true record of events

Date/Time
What happened?

Other related evidence, such as photographs or documents, including where these are stored.

Witnessed by

Signed as a true record of events

Date/Time
What happened?

Other related evidence, such as photographs or documents, including where these are stored.

Witnessed by

Signed as a true record of events

Date/Time
What happened?

Other related evidence, such as photographs or documents, including where these are stored.

Witnessed by

Signed as a true record of events

Date/Time
What happened?

Other related evidence, such as photographs or documents, including where these are stored.

Witnessed by

Signed as a true record of events

Date/Time
What happened?

Other related evidence, such as photographs or documents, including where these are stored.

Witnessed by

Signed as a true record of events

Date/Time
What happened?

Other related evidence, such as photographs or documents, including where these are stored.

Witnessed by

Signed as a true record of events

Date/Time
What happened?

Other related evidence, such as photographs or documents, including where these are stored.

Witnessed by

Signed as a true record of events

Date/Time
What happened?

Other related evidence, such as photographs or documents, including where these are stored.

Witnessed by

Signed as a true record of events

Date/Time
What happened?

Other related evidence, such as photographs or documents, including where these are stored.

Witnessed by

Signed as a true record of events

Date/Time
What happened?

Other related evidence, such as photographs or documents, including where these are stored.

Witnessed by

Signed as a true record of events

Date/Time
What happened?

Other related evidence, such as photographs or documents, including where these are stored.

Witnessed by

Signed as a true record of events

Date/Time
What happened?

Other related evidence, such as photographs or documents, including where these are stored.

Witnessed by

Signed as a true record of events

Date/Time
What happened?

Other related evidence, such as photographs or documents, including where these are stored.

Witnessed by

Signed as a true record of events

Date/Time

What happened?

Other related evidence, such as photographs or documents, including where these are stored.

Witnessed by

Signed as a true record of events

Date/Time
What happened?

Other related evidence, such as photographs or documents, including where these are stored.

Witnessed by

Signed as a true record of events

Date/Time
What happened?

Other related evidence, such as photographs or documents, including where these are stored.

Witnessed by

Signed as a true record of events

Date/Time
What happened?

Other related evidence, such as photographs
or documents, including where these are
stored.

Witnessed by

Signed as a true record of events

Printed in Great Britain
by Amazon